DARTMOOR'S POLICEMAN POET

THE VERSES OF CONSTABLE JOHN L. WEBBER OF WIDECOMBE-IN-THE-MOOR 1863 - 1891

Best wishes

Simon P.

Compiled by Simon Dell, MBE
With a foreword by Sir Roger Birch, CBE QPM

FOREST PUBLISHING

First published in c1878 by Wood & Tozer, Electrical Works, Fore St.,
Devonport

Republished as a new edition in 2000 by FOREST PUBLISHING,
Woodstock, Liverton, Newton Abbot, Devon TQ12 6JJ

British Library Cataloguing in Publication Data

A catalogue record for this book is available from the British Library.

ISBN 0-9536852-1-7

Forest Publishing

Editorial by:
Mike Lang

Typeset, design and layout by:
Simon Dell, MBE

Printed and bound in Great Britain by:
Peter Howell & Co, The Printing Press, 21 Clare Place, Coxside,
Plymouth, Devon PL4 0JW

Cover photographs:
Front - St. Pancras Church, Widecombe-in-the-Moor.
Rear   - The author, Simon Dell, at the Ten Commandments Stones,
Buckland Beacon.

Colour photography by:
Malcolm Sandey, MM

CONTENTS

Page

LIST OF ILLUSTRATIONS

Page

DEDICATION

To the memory of
Constable John L. Webber,
Dartmoor's Policeman Poet.
In the hope that he might approve of his work
being put to such worthy use, helping to restore
St. Pancras Church, where he worshipped.

iv

FOREWORD

As a very young Police Constable 599 of the Devon Constabulary, my sojourn as the village bobby at Widecombe-in-the-Moor was but a brief interlude in a challenging and exciting career. Nevertheless, it was time enough for me to appreciate something of the mystery and magic of Dartmoor and its environs.

My love of this particular part of the moor has never waned and it is easy for me to identify with my illustrious and talented predecessor, John Webber, as he marched his many miles each day about his beat visiting remote hamlets and farms in the isolated parts of the parish. Not much had changed in my day save that I enjoyed the advantage of a bicycle! We both heard the same bells of the lovely Parish Church of St Pancras, albeit tolled by different hands, and we no doubt sheltered under the same wind-swept trees and leaned on the same field gates.

It was on his long walks that John Webber became so well acquainted with the people of this lovely corner of Dartmoor and we are fortunate indeed that he was able to translate so much of his vision into verse, leaving us with an important legacy of the social history of the parish. In 1876 he was a subscriber to a book entitled *Things New and Old concerning the Parish of Widecombe-in-the-Moor and its neighbourhood*, which was published at that time in order to raise funds for the restoration of St. Pancras Church. There can be no doubt that he would have applauded the fact that, over a century later, his poetry is supporting an identical cause.

This book, compiled by a dedicated and equally talented policeman of a more modern age, is a tribute to John Webber, his verse and his love of 'the cathedral of the moor'. Through its purchase you, the reader, have contributed to the restoration of this beautiful church. Thankyou!

Sir Roger Birch, CBE QPM
Former Chief Constable of the Sussex Police.

AUTHOR'S NOTE

John Webber's original paper pamphlet was printed in about 1878 by Wood & Tozer of Devonport, Plymouth. Unfortunately their works was destroyed during the blitz of Plymouth in the early 1940s and was never to be rebuilt. Extensive research and enquiry has failed to identify any particular individual who might be the legitimate copyright holder to Webber's work. Nevertheless, whilst understanding that copyright for the written word lies with the author until seventy years after his death, it is hoped that after such a considerable passage of time no transgression of copyright law has been committed. If, inadvertently, a breach has been committed against any legitimate holder an apology is offered in advance, in the hope that publishing Webber's works in order to raise funds to repair the fabric of a church that he loved is sufficient reason to excuse such an error.

The exact spelling and punctuation of Webber's works have been faithfully reproduced as they were printed over 120 years ago - 'warts and all'!

ACKNOWLEDGEMENTS

The assistance of the staff at the Westcountry Studies Library in Exeter in allowing me to view Webber's original pamphlet has been invaluable. Likewise my thanks are offered to my friend and colleague Alan Leigh for his time and effort in researching Webber's family history for me. Special thanks go to Tony Beard of Widecombe-in-the-Moor for the motivation and inspiration to undertake such a project in the first place, and also to the generous financial sponsors who made the production of this book possible.

INTRODUCTION

A chance conversation at Widecombe-in-the-Moor one evening with Tony Beard, *BBC Radio Devon* broadcaster and local resident of the village, provided the inspiration for this small book. "Have you ever heard of our policeman poet?" he asked. An interesting question because neither I, nor it seems many of the respected authorities on Dartmoor, had ever heard of Constable John Webber, the officer in question. "Some proper stuff he wrote", Tony exclaimed in his inimitable broad Devonshire dialect. This intrigued me no end, and eventually resulted, some weeks later, in a trip to Exeter in order to view the sole printed copy of Webber's poetry that I knew of. I found that Constable Webber had written verses relating to his work, the village, its people and, especially, the churches of both Widecombe and nearby Leusdon.

Tony had explained that the church tower of St. Pancras, at Widecombe, was unfortunately in much need of restoration, costing to the tune of many thousands of pounds, and browsing through the pages of Webber's small pamphlet clearly indicated his own passion for this church as well as the village. Perhaps, in publishing his verses well over a century since he wrote them, some pleasure might be derived from them, and, by donating the profits from the sales of this book to the church tower appeal fund, his works might provide some much-needed financial support to the restoration of the church that he was so fond of. Thankyou for your contribution and support to that worthy project.

Simon Dell, MBE
Police Constable
Tavistock
November 2000

A Devon Constabulary Sergeant and Constables, circa 1871.
A pencil sketch of a sergeant and three constables of the
Devon Constabulary at the time when John Webber was stationed
at Widecombe; showing the canvas backpack used to carry the
constable's equipment on his long marches about his 'beat',
and the low-crowned hat used before the traditional helmet
was introduced in the 1880s.

POEMS

ON

WIDECOMBE-IN-THE-MOOR

AND NEIGHBOURHOOD,

WRITTEN BY

JOHN L. WEBBER,

(THE DARTMOOR POET)

PRICE SIXPENCE

Printed and Published by
WOOD & TOZER, Electrical Works, Fore St., Devonport

Overleaf:

*A reproduction of the original front cover of
John Webber's 58 page pamphlet of poetry
published and printed in about 1878
by WOOD & TOZER, Electrical Works,
Fore Street, Devonport, Plymouth.*

*Their printing works was destroyed during the
wartime blitz on the nearby Devonport Dockyard,
which obliterated most of Fore Street, and was
never to be rebuilt.*

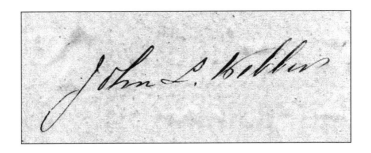

Above:

*The signature of Constable John L. Webber,
taken from his copy of 'Things New and Old
concerning the Parish of Widecombe-in-the-Moor
and its neighbourhood'.*

POETRY ON
Widecombe in the Moor
By JOHN L. WEBBER,
(The Dartmoor Poet)

*I*n eighteen hundred sixty two
On a fine summer day,
And in the month of August too,
I promptly did obey.

An order from our Noble Chief,
Orders we must obey;
From Old Exeter, our depôt,
I soon steamed on my way.

To that wild and dreary region
On th' borders of Dartmoor,
There to take the duties of my station,
Protecting rich and poor.

Fourteen years I've been stationed here
And here I still remain,
And underneath I tell you there
What I have heard and seen.

Six miles north-west from Ashburton,
That fallen old Borough Town,
And three miles from that mansion grand,
Where **BASTARD'S** name resounds.

May be found a village lonely,
Falling down to decay,
Which tells of times destroying hand,
By crumbling walls so grey.

In this parish of wild Widecombe,
Romantic, long, and wide,
Leaves here traces of the Druids,
Old Britons, too, besides.

To tell us tales of what they were,
Think how they lived and died;
There in those circle huts so near,
They lived there tribe by tribe.

Those circle huts so numerous,
And trenches too besides,
And large mounds composed of earthworks
Wherein their dead are laid.

Perhaps died without once thinking,
Or knowing **JESUS'** Name,
Who hung and died through suffering,
Upon that Cross of shame.

On Corndon Tor may now be seen,
The relics of a chair,
In which King Baal sat worshipping
The rock, they call Bel Tor.

Should the Antiquarian direct
His steps toward the moor,
His travels he will ne'er regret,
When travelling days are o'er.

The tourist and the traveller,
They come from far and near,
For health-sake and for pleasure, here,
Each one can have his share.

Not only works thrown up of old
By men so rude and rare;
Here's Nature's work, one may behold,
No finger put it there.

On the wild region of the moor,
Nature's work may be seen,
In th' precincts of Widecombe are
Bold tors, rivulet, and stream.

Rocks, hills and dales, and flowery fields
And meadows looking green,
Watered by God's kind hand, it yields
To us its golden grain.

And those majestic tors so bold,
That look so grand and gray,
Tells tales of dreary nights, so cold,
For ever past away.

Here they have stood for ages past
And will when we are gone;
When we are faded like the grass
And laid low in the mound.

They are speaking of the changing,
In farm and cot below,
And grim death is always raging,
Plays havoc where he goes.

The rippling stream, how swift and fast
We much from him may learn;
Greets farewell to all as he pass,
Never more to return.

The bird that soared high in the air,
Above its lofty head
Is gone forever tho' once near
And numbered with the dead.

Just where two Manors intersect,
South-east of th' village green
If the traveller his steps direct,
God's work there may be seen.

The Nutcracker, or Logan Stone
Surprises human mind;
How that huge block came there its known
No man could ever find.

No man could ever put it there
In the rude state it's in,
Yet I myself have logge'd it there
It is so easily done.

This block of stone contains the weight
One hundred and ten tons,
And yet may be made to vibrate
With the staff six feet long.

North Hall, a mansion house so grand,
And near the village green,
And on an eminence did stand
Surrounded by a stream.

North Hall was then the Manor House,
A place of high renown,
Protected by a water course
O'er which a bridge was drawn.

A water course it may be called,
In other words a moat,
Full ten feet deep and twenty broad
Fed by a gentle brook.

This Mansion House then built so strong,
Arched doors with iron bands,
Where th' **ANDREW** family lived so long
Inside that Mansion grand.

One hundred years ago and more,
I have been told as such,
The **ANDREW** name in days of yore
Was then respected much.

Respected, yet he must be bred
A very wicked one,
A Fox into the Church he led
While service being on.

When reminded by the Vicar
In th' law he'd made a breach,
Said, "the Fox already knew his prayers
And now would learn to preach."

The stately oak, the elm tree tall
And box tree ever green
Was once a pleasing sight to all,
On North Halls ancient scene.

There was the grand arched avenue
And holly always green,
The yew tree, and the laurel too,
All adding to the scene.

A large Rookery was also there
As finish to the scene;
Cawing rooks, no one could number
When they were on the wing.

This mansion once so grand and gay,
No trace can now be found;
The Bridge, the Moat, gone to decay,
That did this house surround.

The stately oak, the elm tree tall,
There saw their infant day:-
Grew on, at last a victim fell
By time that brings decay.

The weeping willow, yew tree too,
Would there in silence weep,
O'er those departing inmates who
Grim death, has called to sleep.

That ancient loft bird, the Rook,
True to its home would be,
She from that place her flight has took,
Never more there to be.

Those ancient ones who once lived there
Their footprints all defaced,
Worn out by time, or grass grown o'er,
No one can find a trace.

Th' King of North Hall, I've heard would scound
The beggar from his door;
Of such by some I've heard the sound,
'Twas true in days of yore.

The Crown has left the Kingly brow,
The staff the beggar's hand
Laid low, moulding together now,
Before one judge must stand.

Death comes to all we plainly read
In spite of all our powers,
The tall, the wise, the Reverend head
Must lie as low as ours.

Should a friend or any stranger
Determine and decide,
To explore, Widecombe's broadacres,
Should there employ a guide.

Let headquarters be, wild Widecombe,
On Monday make a tour,
First, direct your steps to Southcombe,
From there, to the wild Moor.

On the Manor of wild Widecombe,
As you climb the' craggy steep,
A homestead, neat and modern,
Stands out so prominent.

You climb th' steep from Widecombe, to where
Two Lordly Manors meet,
On th' sunny slopes of Southcombe, there
Stands now a family seat.

The home of an ancient family,
Their name and fame so great
Has been, for near three centuries,
Down to the present date.

Southcombe, the home of the **HANNAFORD**,
Who have held their title rights,
Lords of, more than few broadacres,
And still holders of th' rights.

I, like many, was familiar
With that brave stalwart man
John, the father, and grandsire
Of those the present ones.

Some might think him peculiar,
His deportment so sedate,
But approach him near and nearer,
He was man, every wit.

Though, so few among the thousand
In th' human race of man,
That will do th' right and speak the same
Toward his fellow man.

He possessed th' different attributes,
That he attained unto
Versed in th' laws of England's statute,
But, th' laws of **GOD** more so.

The family lives now, tho' diminished,
Here's one now at Southcombe,
In th' garden mid the wilderness,
Seated in th' family home.

Let all rejoice until th' finish,
For their example shown,
Only man without a blemish
May at them cast a stone.

Then ascend up, high and higher,
To the summit of the hill,
Crowned with cragged rocks and heather,
So ghastly, all so still.

Then go on yet far and further,
No voice, but all a glare
Only th' warbling of some songster,
As he mounts in the air.

Then glance o'er the landscape yonder,
But only here and there
A homestead of some farmer,
Or cottage rude and rare.

There's old ancient Blackdon Manor,
Where lived, long, long ago,
Many rude and ancient dweller,
In th' dark days long ago.

Then go on towards old Grendon,
Nestled on a gentle slope,
Where th' name of **IRISH**, so well known
For lasting good repute.

Then ascent up high and higher,
Above the gentle slope,
There's th' seat of one so familiar,
Well know as, Cator Court.

A neat little homely mansion,
And one of modern style
Stands in th' flowery, shrubbery garden,
Wherein lived th' honoured squire.

FIRTH, th' lord of Cator Manor,
And Manor House complete,
A Manor within the Manor,
The Manor of Spikewyk.

Gentleman in reality
Without a doubt, by birth,
Perhaps from noble Scotch family,
May be, the Firth of Firth.

Be as it may from whom he sprung,
By all was lov'd most dear,
His duties first to **GOD**, then th' man,
Has made his title clear.

When on the Magisterial bench,
Pattern, none can deny,
Though he's departed and gone hence,
Name of Firth will ne'er die.

Perhaps you go a little further,
Beyond the Cator bounds,
Only th' lark or whistling plover,
Gives you a cheerful sound.

Wind you way back from whence you came,
By way of Cator gate,
Pause, there stands old ancient Riddon,
Within the Duchy right.

Then look round and further, yonder,
And on th' wild region gaze,
The eye piercing far and further,
All wonder and amaze.

On th' way back, you may see nestling
On some rude lonely spot,
Some old farm, weather beaten
Or isolated cot.

Monday, and first day's tour over,
Think on self, likewise th' guide;
Support th' needs of human nature,
Whilst now it's eventide.

When Tuesday morn dispels th' darkness,
You with your fellow guide,
Go see more of Widecombe's wildness,
So ghastly, grim, and wide.

First direct your steps to Lynchford,
Surroundings rude and rare,
The birthplace and home of **CAUNTER**,
For two centuries or near.

Here on the Halt, pause and ponder,
Ov'r that old rustic bridge,
Dates back, showing the inquirer,
Sixteen sixty six.

I'm told when they th' bridge was building,
Something very dire occurred,
A man assisting th' building
Then, who's surname was **FORD**.

He, for that offence so direful,
Was caught and lynch'd to death,
There part way up on Lynchford hill,
Suffer'd that dreadful death.

With the guide move up, and higher
On the gorse and heathered sward.
It becomes more wild and wilder,
To th' north, east, or westward.

There's the Convict Prison yonder,
Standing on th' gentle slope,
That fills tender hearts with horror
To think, of th' crimes and guilt.

Unless th' eye strain'd by far reaching,
Or th' brain turned by deep thought,
Look, the ghastly diresome building,
Grows wilder as you look.

That Castle of ghastly horror,
With hundreds vile and base,
Both th' villian and the murderer,
They of England's fallen race.

Then down, down the cragged hillside,
By th' winding road so steep,
In th' valley neath the hillside,
There th' east and west Dart meet.

There the two meet one the other,
And join one another,
And on they both together,
Towards a deep ravine.

Now united each to either,
None can part nor sever,
They go on laughingly together,
Into the deep ravine.

Look to one side or the other,
Frightful altogether,
Cragged hillsides clad with heather,
Is th' ghastly deep ravine.

Over rocks and round the boulder,
Waters deep and broader
Making solemn dismal murmurs
As they pass th' deep ravine.

Tuesday's sun is sinking yonder,
Night is drawing nearer,
Calling on Widecombe's traveller
Return, it's eventide.

Then wind your way back together,
Before th' darkness gather,
To the place at where you quarter,
The traveller and the guide.

Wednesday morning tour together,
Atmosphere in favour
Then direct your footsteps thither,
To Buckland in the moor.

Within th' limits of that Manor,
Ancient altogether,
Where many a barder dweller,
Lived there, long, long ago.

Travel on a little further,
Then you pause and ponder,
Here's the seat of England's warrior,
When at Sebastopol.

BASTARD, lord of Buckland Manor,
Kind heart'd altogether,
Tho' he was , soldier, officer,
Now, Buckland's honour'd squire.

In that mansion quite a picture,
Extoll'd for its grandeur;
Lived Briton's retired warrior,
Now th' loved and honour'd squire.

Having viewed the landscape over,
And admir'd its grandeur,
On th' summit, just up yonder,
Stands th' people's house of prayer.

A small plain and ancient structure,
Meaning deep in figure,
In the centre of God's acre,
Stands the old house of prayer.

Having now seen th' exterior,
And admired with pleasure,
Then next view the interior,
The traveller with his guide.

Then here now and no longer linger,
And without a murmur,
Down through th' darksome woods together,
To where th' two Webburs meet.

Previous they have been assunder,
Not known each to other,
But here they embrace each other,
At th' place call'd Lizwell meet.

Here, traveller and guide together
Should sit down and ponder,
Perhaps with a shuddering horror, where
East and west Webburn meet.

That ravine fills th' one with terror,
Ghastly altogether,
Look to one side or the other,
Ghastly, wherev'r you look.

But they both go on together,
Without th' gloom or terror,
Through the zigzag course they murmur
We are near our friend th' Dart.

With full speed, from fast to faster,
Round the nook and corner,
Near th' bridge, to me familiar,
They plunge into the Dart.

Here the four combine together,
Stronger now than ever,
Grow more haughty and more prouder,
As they journey to the sea.

Human power can never hinder,
Farewell th' barder dweller,
To return again, no never,
Our home is in the sea.

At the bay near Dartmouth Harbour,
Their wild journey over,
There they bid farewell for ever,
And plunge into the sea.

Wednesday's tiresome journey over,
Wind you way together
Back, rejoicing ov'r the grandeur,
The traveller and the guide.

Thursday morning, breaks on Widecombe,
And th' lark is mounting high,
Take advantage of the morning,
And view the landscape wide.

Of that lordly Manor, Widecombe,
Through which east Webburn flows,
Then ascend the hill so irksome,
Bath'd in the morning dew.

Up the slope towards great Northway,
Old homesteads here and there,
Lived th' far farm'd family, **NOSWORTHY**,
For centuries, or near.

Their good name and reputation,
Both, so greatly esteem'd,
For so many generations,
And to day remain th' same.

The guide may inform th' traveller,
Something of their repute,
Their morals of good character,
Not one, may dare dispute.

Their sayings, yea, and their doings,
Obedient to the law,
I'm not aware if, a victim,
To England's statute laws.

Then up Widecombe's hill, yet higher,
Informed perhaps by your guide,
That once lived a barder dweller,
On Bonhill's sunny side.

Amid granite rocks and boulders,
Looking so grim and gray,
Stood th' home of an ancient dweller,
Of seventeenth century.

That old ancient barder, **HAMLYN,**
Whose son had strayed away,
To another sphere of action,
Wander'd to Buckfastleigh.

Lived in an humble cottage, near
The far farm'd river Dart,
Sought employment with a weaver,
And to fortune made th' start.

With diligence and earnestness,
Combined with power of brain,
Soon became partner in th' business,
And shared th' losses and th' gain.

From one step on to another,
They very soon embarked
On the business, as a Tanner,
And hand mill to grind the bark.

At last th' comb, th' loom, the old bark mill
Became hidden in th' dark,
Now it's a wheel within a wheel,
Each wheel takes his own part.

I've been told, he th' barder dweller,
Said I will th' lesson teach,
Walk from Bonhill into Cornwall,
And hear John Wesley preach.

For walking, there was scarce a match
For this pedestrian,
Walked, to Bodmin, hear Wesley preach,
From there walked back again.

What a marvellous example,
Have th' **HAMLYN** family shown,
From Bonhill's barder dweller,
To fortune and to fame.

Having now informed the traveller,
Of th' family so antique,
Climb the hillside crown'd with heather,
Then to Hennsbury Gate.

Near, and not far from the roadside
Is there, a more antique
A circle, round which, side by side,
Where seven lords' lands meet.

First, is that of Mr **HARPER**
Holwell, his family seat;
Second, lord **CRAUNSTOWN** of Baytor,
Third, th' duke of Somerset.

Fourth, **J. WOODLEY**, of Halshanger,
An honour'd Magistrate,
Fifth, **BASTARD** of Buckland Manor,
Man of such high repute.

Sixth, **R. DYMOND**, lord of Blackslade,
And Duston too as well;
Seventh, is that of Mrs **DRAKE**,
By hundreds known full well.

Having now informed th' traveller,
The place where these lords meet,
Place of abode, and who they were,
But some have fallen asleep.

Now pass on a little further,
And to another stage,
To th' summit over yonder,
Near Tunhill and Blackslade.

Near the roadway, down the hillside,
By th' guide you may be shown,
Near the Manor House of Blackslade,
A coffin made of stone.

I've seen this old ancient relic,
To others I have shown,
This old coffin, all but perfect,
Only needs th' cover stone.

I have taken its dimension,
Its length, its width, and depth,
From north to south, it's four feet long,
Two feet in width and depth.

A chest of th' remote ancestor,
Who once lived there and died,
Buried in that stone sepulchre,
Perhaps th' King of his own tribe.

Now cease th' travels, day is over,
Evening is drawing nigh,
Down the slope to where you quarter
Yourself, and weary guide.

Friday morning rouse th' traveller
From th' slumbers and his sleep,
And direct his footsteps thither
To th' Manor of Spitchwick.

Through the hamlet that is Dunston,
Records an ancient type,
Where lived those **HEXT** and **HAMLYN**,
In eighteen sixty eight.

HAMLYN an old border dweller,
One of the olden type,
An old yeoman and freeholder,
Lived on his own estate.

He conversant and familiar,
Was most intelligent,
Although fourscore years or older,
His sayings nice and quaint.

I have heard him boast the grandeur,
When in his company,
They were lords of Dunston Manor,
When Cromwell had the sway.

They were the most ancient family,
In Widecombe of to day,
Dates back to the sixteenth century,
When wealthy then were they.

HEXT, they too were Dunston dwellers,
Of ancient pedigree,
Also yeomen and freeholders,
In seventeenth century.

HEXT, **HAMLYN**, became united,
By lawful marriage ties,
Heritage became divided,
On few had brought surprise.

At th' bottom of th' green yonder,
Stands the old Manor House,
Where lived the lords of Dunston Manor,
In th' reign of James the first.

Within this old gothic structure,
The **HAMLYN'S** would reside;
HEXT'S of late have followed after,
But gathered up and died.

Let historian or th' stranger,
For th' purpose of research,
Pause o'er this old gothic structure
With its sharp pointed arch.

I'm told by both **HEXT** and **HAMLYN**,
Of that huge granite block,
That stands in Dunston Village Green,
Had a basin on th' top.

Manor Courts were formerly held there,
Some sat round, some on th' top,
Chief rents and dues deposit there,
In th' hewn basin on th' rock.

They likewise informed me further,
Of th' relic they had lost,
That stood near that massive boulder -
'Twas an old Roman cross.

But th' Vicar, Mr **MASON**, came
And carted it away,
Placed it in the Vicarage garden,
Without the yea, or nay

Having now inform'd th' traveller,
Of Dunston's pedigree;
The parts and the fragments gather'd,
Gives me authority.

Now proceed a little further,
By scatter'd farm and cot,
Just a little over yonder,
At th' barton make a stop.

Where lived **MANN**, th' life-long preacher,
Where he first learn'd, has taught,
And wrote it so indelible,
Will not soon be forgot.

His example was the preacher
At home, at any place
Would be mindful, and with hammer
Drive th' nail in a sure place.

Perhaps th' friend, or any neighbour
Who pass through, or by th' gate
Hear from th' seat of thought a whisper,
He has done and spoke th' right.

Although dead may be a preacher,
There remains th' still small voice,
Wafted back from over yonder,
Go, thou, and do likewise.

Through the Barton, by the footway,
And onwards as you glide;
There's relics of antiquity
In front, and either side.

As you cross east Webburn over,
Where th' Mill stands by its side,
Perhaps you climb the hillside higher,
If encouraged by th' guide.

Here's Stone House, where lived a unit
Of the **ANDREW** family,
Now extinct, then so prolific
In seventeenth century.

This historic ancient building,
So old and so remote,
Four centuries or more standing
There, none will ever doubt.

Should a paragraph be written
On its antiquity,
By traveller or historian,
Should the interior see.

Mark there the striking interest,
And its old tracery,
And the old winding stone staircase -
Each step ten inches high.

Now gloomy and all deserted,
Fallen down to decay,
Once a place of note and noted,
When Cromwell had the sway.

Where lived **ANDREWS** in their grandeur,
With glad hearts full of mirth,
Have return'd into **GOD'S** acre
Earth, to its mother earth.

NORRISH too has followed after,
The chain had many links,
But all have been snapped asunder,
And here become extinct.

By permission go together,
The traveller with his guide,
Through the Buckland Woods, you wander
By th' winding zig zag drive.

Having no desire whatever,
Your footsteps to retrieve,
Those romantic works of nature,
No stranger can conceive.

Now on to old Spitchwick Manor,
A place of high renown,
And historic fragments gather,
Here's many to be found.

Enter by the Lodge together,
The traveller and his guide,
Through the avenue of grandeur,
Wooded on either side.

Remind th' traveller while together,
This drive was opened out,
Substituted for another,
Back in days more remote.

I was informed in sixty-four
By one that who had been
A domestic at Spitchwick, for
That honour'd man Squire King.

She was near, or nearing eighty,
When she the statement made,
That the avenue so stately
Had trees on either side.

From one Lodge to the other,
Which is a measur'd mile,
Might take th' naked candle over,
And burning all the while.

Ascend th' winding drive, yet higher
You confront th' entrance gate,
To that ancient noble structure -
The mansion of Spitchwick.

Here you look with admiration
On th' mansion, grand, and great
With its picturesque surroundings
So old, and so antique.

'Twas the seat of one **JOHN DUNNING**,
Perhaps some are well aware,
In the Grammar School, Ashburton,
When young, he studied there.

A shred man was he, **JOHN DUNNING**,
Soon became th' barrister,
Created Baron Ashburton,
From lawyer to a peer.

That brilliant star of Ashburton,
Altho' a peer was he,
Died at Exmouth, in th' County Devon,
In seventeen eighty three.

Near the mansion of old Spitchwick,
Stood an old Chapel, where
Many ancestors have worshipp'd
And bowed in homage there.

I've seen some fragments of th' building
Lying by th' garden wall,
Behind that old stately mansion,
Some in parts, others whole.

Preserved there by **WM. KITSON**,
The loved and honour'd squire,
Where he, lord, and in possession
Of th' stately mansion there.

Relics of the Church St. Leonard,
Of thirteenth century,
But fallen, ruined and demolished
Now, is that old chantry.

The guide should escort the traveller,
Historian in disguise,
To lower town, substituted for,
The old name - Christians Hays.

There stands an old antique building,
Once known as Christians Hays,
Where lived then the Priest, or Deacon,
Of St. Leonard Church of ease.

The owner of this old building,
Is th' well known Mr. **CLEAVE**;
Lives in this old priestly Mansion,
What once was Christians Hays.

Now climb on to Luesdon's summit,
View th' landscape far and near;
On the slopes you may see dotted,
Old homesteads here and there.

Where a unit or an offspring,
Of remote family,
Here's the **HANNAFORD** and **HAMLYN**,
Of sixteenth century.

At Lower Ash, there lived a unit,
Or link in th' family chain;
HAMLYN, in sixteen fifty six,
Lived there in Cromwell's time.

At Lake, in th' same locality,
One more link in th' chain,
There **HAMLYN** owned, and occupied
In sixteen sixty one.

Climb the cragged hillside higher,
To that of Lower Tor;
For the oldness of the structure,
Historian would admire.

Lives an offspring of th' **HANNAFORD**,
Who for two centuries,
In Widecombe, they have been noted
For their integrity.

Let this end the Friday's labour,
As now it's evening tide,
With glad hearts return to quarter,
And there rest satisfied.

Saturday, once more together,
On the last working day,
Perhaps forget th' voice of preacher,
That all is vanity.

Then up Widecombe's Vale together,
Where stands th' far famed Wooder,
Where the lord of Widecombe's Manor
Gather'd up th' feet and died.

The guide may there in a whisper,
Unfold in some measure,
That she was eccentric creature,
But worse have lived and died.

Mrs. **DRAKE**, some may remember,
When lady of th' Manor,
Was friend to butcher and th' brewer,
Yea, many more besides.

She would welcome any stranger,
Male, or female either,
And render to th' beggar,
Her hospitality.

Her heart would extend yet further,
Than man, th' woman either
Always merciful, and tender
To th' quadruped was she.

Now extend your footsteps further,
With the guide as leader,
On to Notsworthy old Manor,
With its wild scenery.

You may here stop, pause, and ponder,
From the guide you gather,
There stands Bonhill over yonder,
Of ancient pedigree.

For three centuries and over,
SMERDON'S have been th' owners,
But of late it has turned over
To th' late **MARK KENNAWAY**.

These old ancient barder dwellers,
Wealthy, and the land owners,
For three hundred years and over,
Since fifteen fifty three.

Climb the mountain steep, yet higher,
With determined vigour,
To raven rock, th' massive boulder,
So ghastly, grim and gray.

Rich green ivy in a cluster,
Round this massive boulder,
Where th' raven builds th' nest for shelter,
Until her young can fly.

That ancient bird so singular,
Strangers there have watch'd her,
Round the rock, would see her hover,
And hear the young ones cry.

The guide may escort the traveller,
'Mid that wild scenery,
Within th' limits of the Manor,
The far fam'd Notsworthy.

Where the huge gigantic boulders,
Stands there so rude and crag'd,
Such a wild picture to th' stranger
Are those of honey bag.

With a frightful admiration,
Of this wild scenery,
Fifteen hundred feet you're standing,
Above the dark blue sea.

Now proceed a little further,
To th' modern mansion grand,
Where lived th' Manor's lord, SQUIRE TUCKER.
So dignified a man.

He was always so complaisant,
As far as I have seen,
From his equals down to peasant,
Was loved by every one.

Loved by all for his good morals,
Would lend the helping hand,
If he thought some good would follow,
From th' which it was designed.

In the Church stands a monument
In lasting memory,
The pulpit, a grand ornament
By him presented free.

Hewn from those old granite boulders,
So rugged, rude, and gray,
On Hamildon in the Manor,
That of old Notsworthy.

Having view'd the wilds of Notsworthy,
With hills, and dales, and dells,
To describe how wild th' scenery,
No tongue can ever tell.

Having explored Widecombe's wildness,
And now it's evening tide,
Return before the darkness gather,
To quarters with your guide.

Traveller and his guide together,
Hearts filled with thankfulness,
Pause, it's Sabbath on the morrow,
That glorious day of rest.

When the Sabbath breaks on Widecombe,
Sweetly sings the lark on high,
Silence of the day is broken,
From th' sound that's wafted by.

Hark, the bells, it is the Sabbath,
Now to **GOD'S** house repair,
Respond to **GOD** of Sabbath,
And pay due homage there.

Where many a barder dweller,
Have responded to th' call,
Now, traveller and guide together,
Learn th' grand secret of th' bells.

Pray, each and all, with heart and mind,
When at the throne of grace,
GOD save our King, **GOD** save our Queen,
Given them eternal rest.

Widecombe-in-the-Moor Police House.

A photograph of the old police cottage occupied by Webber and his family. This was situated at Bittleford, a short distance from Widecombe, but was demolished shortly after this photograph was taken in the early 1920s.

A FAITHFUL DOG

The dog, a faithful animal,
Obeys his master's word,
Is pleased from him to hear a call,
Or say to him, "Forward."

In eighteen hundred seventy-four,
On a bright summer day,
A man on Dartmoor called his dog
To keep him company.

Beyond the days in all the week
He chose the Sunday for
Some pleasure, or his cattle seek,
He strolled on the wild moor.

Onward they walk together, now
Near Vitaford old mine,
Where furze and fern and heather grew,
The dog was close behind.

When suddenly the furze and fern,
And heather too, gave way;
Master went down, his bowels yearn,
Twenty-five feet deep, they say.

Down at the bottom of the shaft,
That dark and dreary place,
He must have died, had he been left;
The dog showed faithfulness.

41

There on the brink he sat, and heard
His master cry for help;
He sat there, never left the spot
Until next day appeared.

Sat howling, barking all the time,
When th' attention of some friend
Was drawn towards Vitaford Mine,
Where master was fallen in.

A ladder then was soon procured,
And let down in the place,
And master of the dog rescued,
By its most faithfulness.

The rescued man was **HANNAFORD**,
A man I knew full well,
When from his lips I had th' words,
A tear in th' eye would dwell.

Let each and all consider this,
Learn to be good and kind,
And show forth that loving kindness
To th' dumb of any kind.

Man, saved from dreadful wretchedness,
Where would have been his grave?
Only by poor dog's faithfulness,
From th' jaws of death was saved.

THE CHURCH
St. PANCRAS

he Church with her ancient portals,
That glorious place of wonder,
Built on a gentle eminence
In some long forgotten day,
By Ancient ones so dutiful;
No one knows the name of founder,
Perhaps lying near there sleeping,
Waiting, the last great day,
And triumphant Arch there standing
At th' west end in silence speaking,
Pass on, join in prayer and praising,
To whom Angel Host adore,
There with Alleluia praise Him,
And in humble prayer implore Him
To set His seal and signet, "thou
Art mine for EVERMORE."

With pillars tall and beautiful,
All told, fourteen is the number,
In two rows in order standing,
Their strength to the roof convey,
A place altogether lovely,
And may be said one of wonder,
Dedicated to St. Pancras,
In th' fourteenth century.
There the two-arch'd doors are swinging,
Toilers one by one are entering,
With hearts being heavy laden,
Full of sorrow, sad, and sore,
There with Alleluia praise Him,
And in humble prayer implore Him,
He will set His seal and signet,
"Thou'rt mine for EVERMORE."

Twelve arches there magnificent,
Gives the living to remember
How earnest then our fathers were,
Who then spared no cost or pain,
All polished granite, beautiful,
May well be said one of wonder,
Is that huge building on th' moor, where
Our fathers worship'd in,
Where God gives a friendly greeting,
Radiance of His love there streaming
Towards all those that worship Him,
And believe and doubt no more,
On the bended knee before Him,
In praise and prayer implore Him,
To set His seal and signet, "thou
Art mine for EVERMORE."

O'er the South Door, as you enter,
I myself can well remember,
A scripture text in florid paint,
Was presented to one's sight,
Those who to this Church would venture,
Might there see in gaudy colour,
Once painted there by ancient hands,
On th' ground of dirty white,
Those weighty words were speaking loud
To each one of their entering,
Trying to arouse each conscience,
As they enter through the door,
Enter in, no longer fear thee,
Tho' dreadful be th' place I tell thee,
Yet here He will prepare thee, for
Your endless **EVERMORE.**

The text that once was o'er the door,
One of the unfathomed Scriptures,
Were words of the old Patriarch,
For our learning they are written,
In painted lines and they were these,
"How dreadful is this place; this is
None other but the house of God,
And this is th' gate of Heaven."
Now all defaced, those fingers still,
In its Mother Earth lie sleeping,
Those Ancient ones with paint and brush,
Who once wrote o'er the door,
Waiting the last trumpet sounding,
Calling dead ones into waking,
Rise, come forth, receive your sentence,
Lasting for **EVERMORE.**

Then those Ancient ones so dutiful,
Great or small tho' be the number,
Will be ushered in **GOD'S** presence,
By bright Angels on their way,
If they have proved here dutiful,
In this bless'd place of wonder,
Set apart for prayer and praising
Him on St. Pancras Day,
The grave given up her holding,
Now they lie no longer moulding,
But rise to the trumpet's sounding,
Having nothing to deplore,
But enter through th' door that's swinging
And join in the chorus swelling
"Thou'rt always to be with us, through
That endless **EVERMORE**."

This Ancient grand old edifice,
Length, hundred and four feet's th' number,
Its Chancel, Nave, North and South Aisles
Shows forth its Ancient beauty,
Speaks of desertion and decay,
By both rotting roof and rafter,
The green streak walls and rotten pews,
Cry, "All forgotten me."
To the stranger I'm appealing,
As mine they are me deserting,
If I am grand, their hearts are cold,
And they will not me restore,
Shows they are **GOD'S** House forsaking,
Where all true hearts are uniting,
There week by week preparing, for
That endless **EVERMORE**.

Its Chancel and its Chantry aisles,
Style of which is perpendicular,
The Chancel twenty three feet long,
The roof of th' kind of Cradle,
And when restored in sixty eight,
By Carlyon, that worthy Vicar,
O, awful scene, both roof and floor,
And deserted table, -
I witnessed there the rotten scene,
Yea, that solemn place disgraceful,
Where **GOD'S** people together meet,
And feast round that Holy Board,
There by eating and drinking, in
Remembrance of His blood shedding
And by His spirit fitted for
That endless **EVERMORE**.

Among the many features in
This old grand and noble structure,
A portion of Ancient Screen
Painted, colours bright and gay,
The under part of which with care
Has there been preserved in order,
Adorned with Figures still thereon
Shows its Antiquity.
There it still, tho' old, is standing,
Church from Chancel there dividing,
And to all in silence speaking,
In most solemn words implore.
"Enter through by way and welcome,
Ye with heavy hearts and broken
Eat, Drink, He's prepared th' ransom, for
Your endless **EVERMORE**."

The Rood Screen, upper part of which
There once such a noble feature,
Its furniture, embellishments,
So attractive to the eye,
Now disappeared, perhaps broken down,
Or time may have ruled the master,
None left to tell, for all are gone,
Underneath th' sod they lie.
The lower panels still remaining,
Their rich colour still retaining,
Figures of Saints, and not a few,
And one of our **BLESSED LORD**,
Those Saints, who by Faith have found Him,
And in loving fear have served Him,
Are past from Earth to Heaven, in
Their endless **EVERMORE**.

There among those painted figures,
Each and all in their true colours,
Robed in Costume, each setting forth
An emblem of true piety -
There's two Bishops and St. Peter,
Likewise an old Saintly Doctor,
Each and all have washed and made clean
Their Robes in th' crimson dye,
And pass'd through the door that's swinging
Makes no grating, no harsh ringing,
So melodious is the singing
To the **GOD** whom they adore;
And they still the chorus swelling,
Grand beyond a Mortal's telling
The burden of that chorus is -
HOPES glad word **EVERMORE**.

Others representing Martyrs,
Those old faithful fighting soldiers
Who have proved faithful to the end
And for th' cause of Christ have died.
One the figure of St. Stephen,
In conflict none was more bolder,
By false accusers stoned to death,
When dying loudly cried.
He like a true hearted Christian
There prayed they might be forgiven
That nothing be laid to their charge.
He in dying words implored,
When on the cold ground he lying,
A true Martyr, bleeding, dying,
Now fought the fight that's ended in
His happy **EVERMORE**.

Among the above named figures,
May be traced that unbeliever
Thomas, that faithless doubting one
Disbelievingly replied,
Said, "I'm still an unbeliever
Unless I can put my finger
In th' nailprints and then thrust my hand
Into that wounded side."
The eighth day, he still retaining
The same spirit, disbelieving,
When who should enter in their midst
But **JESUS**, through th' fast-closed door
And there spoke in words entreating,
"Be not faithless, but believing,"
The doubting Thomas then believèd,
Had Life for **EVERMORE**.

To leave the subject of the screen
And pass on in silence, ponder,
And pause a while with thinking gaze
Upon the Chancel's beauty,
Carved work with Bosses set thereon
Subjects differ much in figure,
Some of which have disappeared, caused
By time that pass'd them by.
There were figures representing
A Monk and an Ancient Griffin,
Half figure of St. Catherine
Destroyed when th' Church was restored,
But Heads, Leafs, Flowers, Fruits remaining
Though much their colours fading,
Such a solemn sermon preaching
From the word **EVERMORE**.

Pass on to the North Chantry Aisle-
One may there behold the grandeur
A small arch'd door with granite jambs,
Will arrest the gazing eye,
In Gothic style, with winding stairs,
Altogether twelve in number,
Led from Chancel to th' Rood Loft, all
Perfect, each one foot high,
Doorway cleared and its white washing,
A slight treasure there was lying,
Under a mass of rubbish were,
Three small crosses buried there,
Relics fallen to desolation
Speak in silent lamentation,
"Pope and Priest have me forsaken,
Both gone for **EVERMORE**."

One of these old Romish Crosses
Has an incised one in centre
All of which in their rough-hewn state,
Each two feet five inches high
Two Centuries and half or more
Must have lain this hidden treasure
Therein bundled, perhaps offensive,
When Cromwell had the sway.
Till of late this Ancient Building
Partly underwent restoring.
When opened up to public view,
The old staircase and the door,
To us all an insight giving
Then to now, in our believing
Faith in Christ's Blood atoning, we
Have Life for **EVERMORE**.

Of the many different figures
One was there among the number
The Historians would much admire
Could it there preservèd be
It was the youthful St. Pancras,
Under **CHRIST** a valiant soldier
Who died when fourteen years of age
We're told from history
While so gloriously confessing
Underwent that death, beheading,
And inter'd at Calipodius
In three hundred and four,
There at Rome, He will lie sleeping
Till the last great day of reckoning
When myriad friends will cheer him through
That endless **EVERMORE**.

The window of North Chancel Aisle
Still retains a noble figure,
Label of which springs from two heads
At th' point of the Arch is found
Composed of three lights, its tracery
None now in the Church more older,
Fragments of stained glass and a Head
Of th' blessed Virgin crowned
There the figure representing
The one by the **CROSS** there standing
T'was the Virgin Mother weeping
For her dying son, our Lord.
Now with th' blest her voice is tuning
To those golden harps there sounding
Within those golden portals, where
Is gladness **EVERMORE**.

Pass to the South Chancel window,
You, Historian, or the stranger
Note the marks of striking interest
In its double tracery.
Underneath is a priest's doorway,
That time has required surrender
Of late has fallen into disuse
By change and not decay
The Chancel, its floor and railing
Of late undergone restoring
Which blockades th' way of entrance now
Through that Old Gothic Door
For so many ages swinging
And that man of God admitting
Now bolt and bar has made it fast
Perhaps for **EVERMORE**.

In that Holy place, the Chancel,
Was of late two handsome figures
Fronting that holy board was there
Adorned in rich painting gay,
MOSES and **AARON**, so admired
Both by all and every stranger,
Of late broke down and cast aside
No longer there to stay,
By some few of late possessing
Those new fangled notions being
Opposed to their remaining though
Their retention was implored
Which caused many bitter feeling,
Ties of friendship disuniting
Hearts ceased to beat in union, and
Perhaps for **EVERMORE**.

A Handsome Altarpiece was there
Highly extolled for its grandeur,
Tells how the Church was once adorned,
In words speaking soft, but loud
The costly gilding, th' rich painting
Was most elegant in colour,
Representing the sun shining
From underneath a cloud
Broke down after all the striving,
Ornamenting, beautifying,
Disappeared and leaving anger-
That most deadly wound so sore,
Which requires the Blood Atoning
With that Gilead's Balm so healing,
To heal th' deadly wound and fit it
For that long **EVERMORE**.

53

Gone too are those old ochre scrolls
Red and yellow so familiar,
To all in time when gilt and paint
So attracted then the eye;
Those scripture texts daubed on the walls,
In their bright and brilliant colours,
Likewise the English Coat-of-Arms
Has ceased from there to be;
Placed there without once intending
To debase it, or degrading,
But old British taste displaying
Love towards that House of Prayer.
Gone with the past as offending
Are those texts of Bible teaching,
And fingers that once put them there,
All gone for **EVERMORE**.

Gone in the misty cloud of time
Where our thoughts can never wonder
Its th' reading desk that once stood there
In those bygone Ancient days
Because 'twas mean, and not in style,
Having none is much the meaner,
Fanatic notions first condemn'd
Then time hurl'd it away,
Where the Priest in olden time was there
His large congregation leading
Duties performed there as a task
Then so much to be deplor'd
Now gone by is this cold teaching
Which has caused so much dissenting,
Hid in the caverns of the past
In that dark **EVERMORE**.

The Pulpit that of late stood there
So full of decay and danger;
Its design was octagonal
Having its eight equal sides,
Was entered by a flight of steps
And stood by granite pillar,
Panels, each of polished wainscot
One foot six inches wide.
A sound board was overhanging
With the Pulpit harmonizing
Limiting the voice of the preacher,
There between the roof and floor,
On it th' figure representing
An Angel his trumpet sounding,
Figurative or showing forth
That last great **EVERMORE**.

Of all th' striking marks of interest,
One, I feel I dare pass over,
Is the design of the building,
Builded so mysteriously.
Built on the figure of A Cross,
O'er which all should pause and ponder
As it typifies th' **CROSS OF CHRIST**
Once on Mount Calvary.
Come enter the solemn building,
For penitential prayer and praising,
As here is room for all who come
In this Cathedral of th' Moor.
The Spirit and th' Bride entreating
O, let each one say, I'm coming
To worship Him who bled and died,
Now lives for **EVERMORE**.

As time brings change, it brings decay,
To whom man and things surrender
Our Church discipline shows the more
Now in those enlightened days,
The change has caused division here
And love has gave place to anger
By discarding th' grand ornaments
And th' singers gallery;
Where the Bass, Flutes and Fiddles tuning,
To a Choir of forty singing
Anthems and Psalms, in old version,
Sung in union and concord,
Each and all their own part taking,
So melodious was the singing
In loud praise, to Him, who once died,
Now lives for **EVERMORE**.

Why not the time again arrive?
As it's known there's none more grander
Than instruments, they far exceed
Harmoniums in this our day,
If handled well by skilful hands
And under a skilful Leader,
Nothing in a choir will equal
Instruments for melody.
In our churches much is needing
In that part of worship, praising,
As becomes both Priest and people
To join th' praise as in th' prayer
And hear Primitive Church teaching
Then no cause for one's dissenting
But go all as one in union
Towards that **EVERMORE**.

Then cast the sad and gloom away
And look to the bright future
And in that hallow'd place of prayer,
Make the first step on the way;
As there stands the grand Ancient Font,
Its meaning so deep in Figure,
Waiting th' young Lambs to be brought in
God's fold and family,
O, what awful thoughts, how striking,
The negligence in complying
With words, Suffer them to come to
Me, As I am the only door,
Take my Yoke, it's easy wearing,
The Cross on your Brow appearing,
Keep up the warfare that ends in
Your happy **EVERMORE**.

Keep up the fight from infancy,
Perhaps here again you enter
In presence of your leader, for
Whom you fight so manfully,
To covenant yourself afresh,
As it were on oath you enter,
Into contract with some helpmeet,
God has prepared for thee
There at the communion waiting
The arrival of one leaning
On the arm of some bosom friend,
It may be a Father dear,
There they two in one uniting
Their troth each to other plighting,
Twain made one at God's command, till
Death parts for **EVERMORE**.

Then go on ye twain th' two made one,
Gird yourself with the true armour,
The powers of Hell shall not prevail
Against your true gallantry,
Then stand erect, keep in the ranks,
Look to front, obey commander,
Press forward, never fear a scar
Nor courage daunted be
Then forward you the right Brigade,
Clad in all your Armour dazzling
The Helmet, Sword, and Breastplate too,
Fight, the victory is sure,
See His flag and banner waving,
All through life's long conflict raging
When battle o'er the prize is yours,
Cheer, cheer for **EVERMORE**.

The conflict o'er we have the crown,
Perhaps herein again you enter,
For the last time, and silent too,
Weapons of warfare laid aside
In this grand temple of our Lord,
Carried with the dead to slumber
And o'er the lifeless body, is
That solemn service read,
Though cold, dead, and lifeless lying,
Yet in th' unknown world surviving,
No more twain to meet again,
In this Cathedral of th' moor,
Resist not His spirit's striving,
As we all shall soon be lying,
And friends will close th' door and leave us,
And that for **EVERMORE**.

THE TOWER

*A*t the west end of th' Church it stands
On the very place, or near,
Where once stood a more ancient one
Undoubtedly at the rear.

It stands close connected with th' Church
But of more recent date
And if for tracery you search
Nothing will indicate.

A faint style of Sixteenth century
Is there, but not complete,
In the staircase is that tracery,
But not authenticate.

So majestic, tall, and handsome
It stands th' champion of th' moor
And we to day may glory in
Our fathers gone before.

It's been handed down through centuries
That those our fathers were
A tribe of successful miners
Who gave us th' noble Tower.

Another branch, by hundreds,
Were scattered o'er the moor;
They went by the name of streamers
Streaming the valleys o'er.

Tin then being in abundance,
And other costly ore,
To **GOD** they offered in obedience
Part of their golden store.

Both the miners and the streamers,
Inspired by Heavenly grace,
Each drove, as it were with hammer,
A nail in a sure place.

I've seen many gaze and wonder
As to its marvellous height,
But none made attempt to measure,
None could describe its height.

Of all the grand towers in the west
For this one can excel,
But one may be found at Probus,
In th' county of Cornwall.

Its height and design of building,
Similar to that of ours
In all points, but not exceeding
This noble Tower of ours.

In eighteen hundred sixty-four -
The day was bright and fine -
By appointment I met the Vicar,
That man of **GOD** Divine.

He said, "Though th' task be difficult,
We'll struggle hard and try
From door to top of pinnacle,
And ascertain how high."

To th' measuring we proceeded
With plumbob rule and line;
In th' measuring I assisted
The Revd. P. Carlyon.

Now by rule it has been measured -
That no one can deny -
And from floor to top one hundred
And twenty-five feet high.

Now praise **GOD** for their charity,
Ye rich, as well as poor,
And hand down to posterity
"The miners gave the Tower."

St. John The Baptist Church, Leusdon, circa 1899.
An early photograph of the interior of the Church of St. John the Baptist at Leusdon. The inside of the building has changed greatly since Webber's day.

DAUGHTER CHURCH
ST. JOHN THE BAPTIST

*T*he Mother Church at last conceived,
Which caused great surprise and wonder,
But time went on and facts revealed
The birth of a comely daughter.

Early in th' year of sixty-two
On Luesdon Hill Commenced th' labour,
Where crowds assembled (not a few)
With rapturous joys and laughter.

To witness there the great event,
The greatest of the century,
Foundation Stone here duly laid,
On this great and eventful day.

Labour commenced with all fervour,
Urged on with all dexterity;
Men worked hard without a murmur,
And made great progress every day.

After eighteen months' hard labour,
Combined with diligence and care,
Luesdon now can boast the grandeur
In having daughter Church (so fair).

Now born, reared to maturity,
And so complete in every part,
Then for her Consecration Day
June twenty-fourth was set apart.

On this great and eventful day
Was seen a most impressive sight;
The Bishops, likewise the Clergy,
Clad in their emblems of true light.

At Luesdon House they assembled,
And there formed up in rank and file;
From there to the Church proceeded,
The Church, the Mother's Virgin Child.

Headed by th' Bishop and th' Founder,
On th' line of march they trod, offered
What **GOD** had first bestowed on her
She there has rendered back to **GOD**.

That sixty-three, June twenty-fourth,
Will long be had in memory,
When the Right Revd. Bishop Trower
Consecrated and announced it free.

Now set apart by this service
To th' praise and glory of our **GOD**,
Dedicated to St. John th' Baptist,
That Holy, martyr'd saint of **GOD**.

She stands, a noble monument,
As tribute to the memory
Of one always so prominent
In doing good and giving free.

Then laud th' name of Mrs. Larpent,
Let her be honour'd and adored
By all, for this noble present,
This new, grand Temple of our **LORD**.

GOD will also bless His servant
When she has o'er life's journey trod - -
"Well done, good and faithful servant,
Enter into th' joy of thy Lord."

Now come, enter you, **GOD'S** children,
For prayer, and praise your Father **GOD**;
GOD will glory in His children
And children in their father **GOD**.

At the foot of lordly Luesdon,
And where the Dart's bright water's flow,
Worshipp'd many ancient dweller,
In the old Chapel long ago.

Now here stands another Chapel,
Near where the ancient chantry stood,
Shelter'd by the steeps of Luesdon,
Rising from th' ghastly, darksome wood.

See, the morning breaks on Luesdon,
And sweetly sings the lark on high;
Makes the Dart responsive music
As he so laughingly runs by.

When the sun mounts high and higher,
Bathing all in its golden glow,
Up the cragged steeps of Luesdon
Steals a faint sound from far below.

'Tis the Sabbath, and old Luesdon
Hears, from yonder House of Prayer,
On the breeze a welcome wafted,
Come all who will, and worship here.

There hang the caller at th' Chapel,
How it came there none may tell;
Only huge and silent Luesdon
Knows the grand secret of the Bell.

*(**Author's note**: Within the body of Webber's poetry Leusdon is spelt 'Luesdon', and this is faithfully copied here. The modern-day, generally accepted spelling is Leusdon, although 'Luesdon' and even 'Leusden' appear in old writings.)*

LIST AND NAMES OF CLERGY

*T*ime has gone on and told a tale
Of Clergy come and gone
Who have stood firm, truth to reveal,
And make the Gospel known.

Within this hallowed house of prayer
With boldness they have shown
The way, and the will of Master,
Their Master, Three in One.

It's been handed down through centuries
By men as time went on
From their ancient great, great grandsires
To th' latest of their sons.

From those dark days of one thousand
Three hundred ninety-one,
In those days then so turbulent,
In th' second Richard's reign.

Here was a Mr **FISHACRE**
Officiating then,
But exchanged with Mr **MADEFORD**
In th' same King Richard's reign.

PETER DUKE succeeded **MADEFORD**
In fourteen hundred five,
Whose death is not recorded,
Nor how long he survived.

DUKE was followed by **HUGH BICKLEY**
In days so black with sin,
And died about fifteen-thirty,
When Henry th' Eighth was King.

That man, the King, the monster King,
Dyed with the deepest dye,
Dyed in the blackest dye of sin,
That no one can deny.

His bloody, cruel reign of terror
Against all those, Christ-like,
Would burn them or their heads sever,
Few ever had respite.

There was one, Bishop **CRANMER**,
Found favour in his sight,
Who escaped from being murdered
By that Henry the Eighth.

But when he, that King of terror,
Knew th' day was nearing night,
With all speed he sent for **CRANMER**,
That man of God, Christ-like.

That great prelate was just in time,
But found him quite speechless;
Implored the King to give some sign
If he believed in Christ.

Upon hearing which, he squeezed th' hand,
And held it firm and tight,
And died whilst they were hand-in-hand,
The King and the Prelate.

Now we have a faint hope, although
At the eleventh hour,
Heart-changed from black to white as snow
By **GOD'S** Almighty power.

A Mr **BARBER** followed **BICKLEIGH**,
But th' cure he soon resigned;
Like bird of flight he flew away
And left no trace behind.

MAINWARING succeeded **BARBER**,
Who recently resigned,
After a few years' labour, gathered
Up his cold feet and died.

The living then was next bestowed,
In fifteen forty-nine,
On the Revd. Mr. **POLLARD**,
But he had to resign.

Debarr'd of that presentation,
Some one knew why, what for,
Then it fell to Sub-Dean **BLAXTON**
In fifteen fifty-four.

BLAXTON only held the living
For four months in that year;
WRIGHTSWORTH next inherited in
August of the same year.

We may think and talk of **WRIGHTSWORTH**,
What he had to endure
Whilst persisting in the Gospel truth
In fifteen fifty-four.

In the reign full of ghastly terror,
Through that Queen Mary's reign,
Christians old and young beheaded,
Or committed to the flame.

All that reign of bloody terror
That words can not explain,
Devilish, diabolical,
From beginning to th' end.

That saintly Archbishop **CRANMER**,
A man in faith so rich,
In the flames he died, true martyr,
In fifteen fifty-six.

But at last, poor, wretched Mary,
Her spirit took its flight,
Died from that complaint, the dropsy,
In fifteen eighty-eight.

That despotic, wretched monarch,
From whom **GOD'S** grace had flown,
Was not to be found in Europe
Nor in the world was known.

Woman, woman, bloody Mary,
That monarch, England's Queen,
Anathema Maranatha,
Died England's vicious Queen.

Mr. **HICKE** succeeded **WRIGHTSWORTH**
To see th' end of Mary's reign,
And th' morning of Elizabeth
When she commenced her reign.

Labour'd on with new, fresh vigour,
Church having then some rest;
Fifteen-ninety closed his labour
In th' reign of good Queen Bess.

Next came Mr. **CLEMENT ELLIS**
In fifteen ninety-two,
And died in sixteen thirty-six,
Full of years, not a few.

Revd. GEORGE LYDE followed ELLIS
In sixteen thirty-six;
His name lives now, though he has died,
It was so firmly fixed.

It's handed down from then to now,
Now fresh in most men's minds;
His time was spent in care and cure
Of souls to him consigned.

But at last, in March, th' light went out,
Ended life's little day;
The brittle thread of life was cut
In sixteen seventy-three.

So eminent and eloquent
Was this beloved divine,
To duties of Church Militant
He gave his heart and mind.

Two hundred fifty years have gone
Since he was then divine,
His words and deeds and actions shown
Has caused his light to shine.

I've been informed by many, when
News of their loss was known,
Blinds, from morning until evening
Was on all th' windows drawn.

And on the day of burying,
I'm credibly informed,
Church was filled to overflowing,
There hundreds wept and mourned.

All you to this lone spot are led
To trace the records of the silent dead,
Pause where GEORGE LYDE'S cold ashes sleep,
Whose ardours there have mourned
And weeping willows wept.

JOHN TICKLE followed Revd. LYDE
In sixteen seventy-four,
But to say how he lived or died,
It's not within my power.

In the year of sixteen-ninety,
In th' third King William's reign,
JONATHAN TICKLE fill'd the vacancy
And followed in the train.

Although for thirty years th' Vicar,
I ne'er could ascertain
As to where he went, nor neither
The place from whence he came.

Next came Revd. Mr. HARRIS
In seventeen thirty-three;
His days were few, his years were less,
He only labour'd three.

Next came Revd. Mr. **GRANGER**
In seventeen thirty-six,
Into his long home has entered,
That home for ever fix'd.

Revd. **MARSHALL** followed **GRANGER**
In seventeen eighty-one,
He was zealous, earnest worker
Towards his **GOD** and man.

By his teaching and plain preaching
He made his light to shine,
Gave no cause for once dissenting,
He preach'd the word so plain.

He was only a few years Vicar,
His years were only nine;
I'm told, a more earnest worker
The Church can scarcely find.

Revd. **RENDLE** followed **MARSHALL**
In seventeen ninety-one,
A man always so impartial
Was loved by every one.

What I have heard of that divine
My words can not explain,
But has left th' stamp, good moral man,
As well as that, divine.

All his outdoor life so blameless,
Enriched with godly fear,
Whilst talking of his goodness I've
Seen many drop a tear.

Mr. **MASON** followed **RENDLE**,
And enter'd on the scene
As Vicar, in th' year one thousand
Eight hundred and sixteen.

More than thirty years the Vicar,
But scarcely ever seen
But once a week, then in the Kirk
His visits far between.

In eighteen hundred sixty, so
Ended life's little day,
GOD called for his account, to show
And solve the mystery.

Retired to rest, not complaining,
But th' day was nearing night
He was found a corpse next morning,
Spirit had took its flight.

Mr. **MASON** was succeeded by
The Revd. **P. CARLYON**;
In th' year eighteen hundred sixty
Came this belov'd divine.

A man so full of eloquence,
His preaching, too, so plain;
Tried to rouse the sleeping conscience,
And bring back th' strayed again.

The flock wandered over th' wilderness,
Or driven over the plain,
He tried to prove his faithfulness,
And gather them again.

I've been in that Church on Sunday,
And found so few within;
I numbered, myself inclusive,
Found th' total number ten.

He labour'd on in true earnest
For few years, then resigned;
Accepted the cure at Wisbeach,
And left Widecombe behind.

Then came Revd. **JOHN WILLIAMS**
In eighteen sixty-nine,
Followed that man of eloquence,
The Revd. **P. CARLYON**;

And worked hard with might and vigour,
As did Revd. **CARLYON**,
To seek and search for wanderers.
And bring back th' strayed again.

Those that had been so neglected,
Or th' wolf had took away,
Or some lazy, idle shepherd
Had allowed th' sheep to stray.

I'm a living witness to th' fact,
That Vicar so sublime
Worked hard to keep the sheep he'd got
And care for th' lame and blind.

I have been told times, yea, hundreds,
With glad hearts all aglow;
Gospel light shines bright and brighter
Than fifty years ago.

When they were grovelling in th' darkness,
As dark as any night,
CARLYON and **WILLIAMS** drew th' curtain,
And here let in the light.

No wonder, stumbling in the darkness,
As dark as any night,
If we must have those dark lanterns
Without the oil, or light.

A lantern there for thirty years,
I need not mention name;
Of his talents now we often hear,
But ne'er the good he done.

Although he paid his honest due,
He would not cheat nor wrong,
But as to care and cure of souls,
God's work as left undone.

When Sunday morning came again,
The morn be wind or storm,
In Church again he might be seen
His duties to perform.

Those sacred duties that should be
Performed beyond the rest
Were gone through there most slovenly,
As if it were a jest.

The Sunday o'er his work all done,
Till Sunday comes again,
No visits made by him. It's known,
No word in check of sin.

No little lambs by him was led
In tender pastures, where
Their little souls might there be fed
With food so rich and rare.

No watchful eye kept on the young,
Who are so prone to fall,
And they **GOD'S** ways soon wandered from,
And disobey His call.

The middle age neglected too,
Hearts growing hard in sin;
No saying "Stop, no farther go,
In Hell you'll tumble in."

No bringing back those aged ones,
Their eyes with age grown dim,
But on they went with feeble step,
Likewise with tottering limb.

An instance of faith in Him,
That Holy God Divine,
By whose order comes the sunshine.
Likewise the floods of rain.

Some years ago, in harvest time,
The fields were swamped with rain,
Preventing them from gathering
Their shocks of golden grain.

At last, appeal to him was made,
The worthy clergyman,
A farmer on his Church parade,
There, then accosted him.

Langdon was th' good old farmer's name,
Implored, but all in vain,
To read in Church, for fine weather,
The prayer for which ordained.

"No," was his reply in answer,
For words they were, but true,
What use in Church to read the prayer
While th' wind is where 'tis now?

How cold-hearted, faithless, godless,
Was this sham clergyman;
His heart deficient of God's grace,
No love to God nor man!

Was he a wolf in sheep's clothing?
Each one himself might ask;
Or was he a symbol tinkling,
Or like a sounding brass.

The body to the grave must go,
For what he cared, poor man,
And soul down into Hell might go,
For ever to be damn'd.

On th' last great resurrection morn
Perhaps he'll be horror struck,
And curse the day that he was born,
And th' paps that gave him suck.

Shall our clergy be disgracèd by
Those lamps that fail to burn,
Who from Church drive their flocks away,
And to descent the turn.

It makes the prayerful man exclaim,
"How long, my God, how long?"
And call on His most Holy Name,
"Hasten Thy Kingdom on."

Widecombe Church Tower 1906

The Great Storm of 1638

During the afternoon service on Sunday 21st October 1638 a great storm occurred at Widecombe, and a thunderbolt broke through the roof of St. Pancras Church. This phenomenon left four worshippers dead and injured a further sixty-two.

The event caught the imagination of many, including the Dartmoor poet Noel Carrington (born in Plymouth in 1777), who wrote a verse based on the incident. Another bard, whose literary skills were touched, was the local schoolmaster of Widecombe, one Richard Hill. It was he who wrote a lengthy account of the incident in verse. Whether Roger Hill, who was killed during the storm and whose memorial lies in the church, was some distant ancestor of his is not known, but the lines were inscribed on tablets in the church in commemoration of the event.

They also appeared transcribed in Webber's pamphlet and are reproduced on the following pages, accordingly.

LINES ON A WOODEN TABLET IN THE CHURCH

*I*n token of our thanks to **GOD**,
These tablets are erected,
Who, in a dreadful thunderstorm
Our persons here protected.
Within this Church of Widecombe,
'Mongst many fearful signs,
The manner of it is declared
In these ensuing lines:-
In sixteen hundred thirty eight,
October twenty-first.
On the **LORD'S** day at afternoon,
When people were addressed
To their devotions, in this Church,
While singing here they were
A psalm, distrusting nothing of
The danger then so near,
A crack of thunder suddenly,
With lightning, hail and fire,
Fell on the Church and tower here,
And ran into the choir,
A sulphurous smell came with it,
And the tower strangely rent,
The stones abroad into the air
With violence were sent,
Some broken small as dust or sand,
Some whole as they came out
From the building, and here lay
In places round about.

Some fell upon the Church and brake
The roof in many places;
Men so perplexed were, they knew not
One another's faces;
They all or most were stupified
That with so strange a smell
Or other force, whate'er it was,
Which at that time befell;
One man was struck dead, two were wounded,
So they died a few hours after,
No father could think on his son,
Nor mother mind her daughter,
One man was scorched so that he lived
But fourteen days and died,
Whose clothes were very little burnt,
But many there beside
Were wounded, scorched, and stupified
In that so strange a storm,
Which who had seen would say t'was hard
To have preserved a worm,
The different affections
Of people then were such
That, touching some particulars,
We have omitted much,
But what we have related have
Is truth in most men's mouth,
Some had their skin all over scorched,
Yet no harm in their clothes;
One man had money in his purse,
Which melted was in part,
A key likewise, which hung thereto,
But yet the purse not hurt,
Save only some black holes, so small,

As with a needle made,
Lightning, some say no scabbard hurts,
But breaks and melts the blade,
One man there was sat on the bier
That stood fast by the wall,
The bier was torn with stones that fell,
He had no harm at all,
Not knowing how he thence came forth,
Nor how the bier was torn
Thus in this doleful accident
Great numbers were forborne,
Amongst the rest a little child,
Which scarce knew good from ill,
Was seen to walk amidst the Church
And yet preservèd still.
The greatest admiration was
That most men should be free
Amongst so many dangers here
Which we did hear and see,
The Church within so filled was
With timber, stones, and fire,
That scarce a vacant place was seen
In Church or in the choir,
Nor had we memory to strive
From those things to be gone,
Which would have been but work in vain,
All was so quickly done,
The wit of man could not cast down
So much from off the steeple,
From off the Church's roof, and not
Destroy much of the people;
But He who rules both air and fire,
And other forces all,

Hath us preserved, bless'd be His name,
In that most dreadful fall,
If ever people had a cause
To serve the Lord and pray,
For judgement and deliverance,
Then surely we are they;
Which that we may perform by the
Assistance of His grace,
That we at last in time may have
With Him a dwelling place,
All you that look upon these lines
Of this so sad a story,
Remember who hath you preserved
Ascribe unto His glory
The preservation of your lives,
Who might have lost your breath
When others died, if mercy had
Not step'd twixt you and death,
We hope that they were well prepared,
Although we know not how
'Twas then with them, it's well with you
If you are ready now.

*Amos 4.11 "Ye were as a firebrand plucked
out of the burning."*

JOHN L. WEBBER

John Lake Webber was born in 1832 at Burrington, near South Molton, in North Devon but was descended from a Dartmoor family, his ancestors, up until his grandparents' generation, having lived at Belstone, not far from Okehampton. His father, Henry, was a thatcher by trade and, like his son, had been born at Burrington. His mother, Grace, on the other hand had been born at Chittlehampton, into the Lake family, but when she and Henry had married they had made their home at 'Hillside', Burrington.

John initially followed in his father's footsteps by becoming a thatcher and soon afterwards married Ann Thorne, who had also been born at Burrington, three years before him. Whilst living at Burrington they had a number of children - John (1854), Louisa (1857), Arabella (1859), William (1860) and John Lake Jnr (1862). Sadly, though, two of these children, John and William, both died in 1861 at the ages of six and just seven months respectively.

In the following year, 1862, shortly after the birth of John Lake Jnr, John travelled to Exeter in order to join the Devon Constabulary which had been created in 1856 to replace the centuries-old parish constable system of policing. Then, after completing his training, John was posted to Widecombe-in-the-Moor, a lonely and remote moorland station in the 'E' division, with its divisional headquarters (and senior officer) at Chudleigh, some 10 miles away to the east. Here, John and his family lived at Bittleford, the police house situated just outside the village.

Over the years that followed John and Ann had four more children - Ellen Grace (1864), Henry Arthur (1868), Gertrude Alberta (1873) and Jessie Florence Madeline (1876) - by which time the Church of St. Pancras, Widecombe-in-the-Moor was much in need of restoration and a book entitled *Things New and Old concerning the Parish of Widecombe-in-the-Moor and its neighbourhood* was published in order to raise the necessary funds by sponsorship. In fact, John's name is recorded in that book as having donated ten shillings (50p), a princely sum for a village policeman in 1876. Whether the book, which contained poetry by the well-known Dartmoor poet Jonas Coaker, influenced him at this point is uncertain but, whatever, John took to writing poetry himself shortly afterwards. Then, in 1878, he had his poems printed in a small pamphlet, and whilst his work is not comparable to Coaker's (with whom he would have been acquainted), he does seem keen to speak his mind in some of his forthright verses.

John remained at Widecombe for no less than a quarter of a century in all and eventually retired from the force in 1891; but not before he had lost five more of his children - Jessie (at the age of 5), Gertrude (at the age of 7), Henry (at about the age of 13), Louisa (at the age of 31) and his only remaining son, John Lake Jnr, who had died in 1889 at the age of 27. Knowing his fondness for a church where he saw most of his children buried, and a church which he had supported by donating a considerable sum, it is surely fitting that his own verses - which have lain largely unnoticed for well over a century - should now be published in order to raise funds, once again, for the restoration of the Church of St. Pancras.

History, it seems, repeats itself in the most fitting of ways!